I LOVE TO KEEP MY ROOM CLEAN

أُحِبُّ أَنْ أُرَتِّبَ غُرْفَتِي

Shelley Admont
Illustrated by Sonal Goyal, Sumit Sakhuja

www.kidkiddos.com
support@kidkiddos.com

First edition, 2018

Translated from English by Amal Mrissa
قامت بترجمة هذه القصّة من الإنجليزيّة: أمل مريصة
Arabic editing by Fatima Bekkouche

Library and Archives Canada Cataloguing in Publication Data
I Love to Keep My Room Clean (Arabic Bilingual Edition)/ Shelley Admont
ISBN: 978-1-5259-0872-9 paperback
ISBN: 978-1-5259-0873-6 hardcover
ISBN: 978-1-5259-0871-2 eBook

KidKiddos Books

For those I love the most

لِأَجْلِ أَحِبَّائِي

It was a sunny Saturday morning in a faraway forest. Three bunny brothers had just woken up, when their Mom entered the room.

أَشْرَقَتِ الشَّمْسُ يَوْمَ سَبْتٍ جَميلٍ في غَابَةٍ بَعيدَةٍ . اسْتَيْقَظَ الْأَرَانِبُ الثَّلَاثَةُ مِنْ نَوْمِهِمْ عِنْدَما دَخَلَتْ أُمُّهُمْ إلى الْغُرْفَةِ.

"Good morning, boys," Mom said. "I heard you moving around in here."

قَالَتِ الْأُمُّ : "صَبَاحُ الْخَيْرِ يَا أَوْلَادِ، لَقَدْ سَمِعْتُ صَوْتَ حَرَكَاتِكُمْ مِنْ بَعيدٍ."

"Today is Saturday, we can sleep as late as we want," said the middle brother with a smile.

قَالَ الْأَخُ الْأَوْسَطُ مُبْتَسِمًا : "إنَّهُ يَوْمُ السَّبْتِ ، يُمْكِنُنَا أَنْ نَسْتَيْقِظَ مِنَ النَّوْمِ وَقْتَما نَشَاءُ."

"You can stay in your beds for a while," Mom said, "but I'll have to leave. I need to visit your Granny today. You'll stay with Daddy until I come back."

قَالَت الأُمُّ : " يُمْكِنُكُمْ أَنْ تَقْضُوا مَزيدًا مِنَ الْوَقْتِ على أَسِرّتِكُمْ، و لكِنْ ، عليَّ الذَهابُ لزيارَةِ جدَّتكُمِ الْيَوْمِ، أَمّا أَنتُمْ فَسَتَبقَوْن مع والِدكمْ حتّى أَرْجِعَ ".

"When you get out your beds and brush your teeth, you'll have your breakfast," Mom added. "After that, you can read books or play with your toys. Or, you can go outside and ride your bicycles."

ثُمَّ أَضَافَتْ : "عِنْدَمَا تَنْهَضُونَ، و تُفَرِّشُونَ أَسْنَانَكُمْ، تَنَاوَلُوا فَطُورَ، و بَعْدَ ذَلِكَ، يُمْكِنُكُمْ أَنْ تَقْرَؤُوا كُتُبًا أَوْ تَلْعَبُوا بِأَلْعَابِكُمْ أَوْ تَقُودُوا دَرَّاجَاتِكُمْ خَارِجًا."

"Hooray!" The bunny brothers started to jump on their beds happily.

قَفَزَ الْأَرَانِبُ الثَّلَاثَةُ عَلَى أَسِرَّتِهِمْ مِنْ شِدَّةِ الْفَرَحِ و صَاحُوا : "مرحى!"

"But..." continued Mom, "you are responsible for cleaning your room."

تابعت الْأُمُّ :" وَلَكِنَّكُمْ مَسْؤُولُونَ عَنْ تَنْظِيفِ غُرْفَتِكُمْ."

"When I come back, I want to see this house clean and organized, exactly as it is now. Can you do this?"

"عِنْدَمَا أَعُودُ، أُرِيدُ أَنْ أَجِدَ هَذَا الْبَيْتَ نَظِيفًا و مُرتَّبًا تَمَامًا كَمَا هُوَ الْآنَ. هَلْ تَسْتَطِيعُونَ فِعْلَ هَذَا؟"

"Sure, Mom," answered the oldest brother proudly. "We are big enough and we can be responsible."

أَجَابَ الْأَخُ الْأَكْبَرُ بِفَخْرٍ : "طَبْعًا يَا أُمِّي، نَحْنُ كِبَارٌ و بِإِمْكَانِنَا تَحَمُّلُ الْمَسْؤُولِيَّةِ."

After they brushed their teeth, Dad served a delicious breakfast and an even more delicious dessert. Then the fun began!

بَعْدَ أنْ نَظَّفَ الْأَرَانِبُ أسْنَانَهُمْ، قَدَّمَ لَهُمْ وَالِدُهُمْ فطورًا لذيذًا و حَلَوِيَّات ألَذّ. و بَعْدَ ذَلِكَ بَدَأ الْمَرَحُ!

The bunnies started by putting together their puzzle. Then they continued to their wooden building blocks. Next they turned on the train and played together with the rail trail.

اِسْتَهَلَّ الْأَطْفَالُ مَرَحَهُمْ بِتَرْتِيبِ الْأُحْجِيَةِ، ثُمَّ انْصَرَفُوا إِلَى مُكَعَّباتِهِم الْخَشَبِيَّةِ. بَعْدَ ذَلِكَ قَامُوا بِتَشْغِيلِ الْقِطَارِ و لَعِبُوا مَعًا بِالسِّكَكِ الْحَدِيدِيَّةِ.

"This railway train is my favorite," said Jimmy, the youngest brother, as he flipped the on switch. "This is the best present I've got on my last birthday."

قَالَ أَصْغَرُ الْإِخْوَةِ "جِيمِي" و هُوَ يَنْقُرُ زِرَّ التَّشْغِيلِ : "أَنَا أُحِبُّ اللَّعِبَ بِهَذَا الْقِطَارِ، إِنَّهُ أَفْضَلُ هَدِيَّةٍ قُدِّمَتْ إِلَيَّ في عِيدِ مِيلَادِي."

After playing inside for hours, the bunnies grew bored.

بَعْدَ أَنْ لَعِبَ الْأَرَانِبُ لِبَعْضِ الْوَقْتِ دَاخِلَ الْبَيْتِ، أَحَسُّوا بِالْمَلَلِ.

"Let's go play outside!" said the middle brother, looking out the window.

قَالَ الْأَخُ الْأَوْسَطُ وَ هُوَ يَنْظُرُ مِنْ خِلَالِ النَّافِذَةِ :" فَلْنَلْعَبْ خَارِجًا!"

"Yeah! But we need to clean up here first," said the older brother.

قَالَ الْأَخُ الْأَكْبَرُ :"حَسَنًا! وَ لَكِنْ عَلَيْنَا أَنْ نُرَتِّبَ الْبَيْتَ أَوَّلًا."

"Oh, we have enough time before Mom comes back," answered Jimmy, "we can clean up later." The older brothers agreed and they all went out.

قَالَ جِيمِي :" أُوهْ، لَدَيْنَا مُتَّسَعٌ مِنَ الْوَقْتِ قَبْلَ أَنْ تَرْجِعَ أُمِّي، يُمْكِنُنَا أَنْ نُرَتِّبَ الْمَكَانَ لَاحِقًا." وَافَقَ الْأَخَوَانِ الْأَكْبَرَانِ، ثُمَّ خَرَجَ ثَلَاثَتُهُمْ مِنَ الْبَيْتِ.

Outside, three bunny brothers enjoyed the sunny weather. They rode their bicycles, played hide and seek. Finally they decided to play basketball.

اِسْتَمْتَعَ الْأَرَانِبُ الثَّلَاثَةُ بِالطَّقْسِ الْمُشْمِسِ. رَكِبُوا دَرَّاجَاتِهِمْ و لَعِبُوا لُعْبَةَ الْغُمَيْضَةِ. و أخِيرًا، قَرَّرُوا أَنْ يَلْعَبُوا كُرَةَ السَّلَّةِ.

"We'll need our basketball," said older brother. "But I don't remember where we put it."

قَالَ الْأَخُ الأكبرُ: "نَحْتَاجُ كُرَةَ السَّلَّةِ، و لَكِنَّنِي لَا أَتَذَكَّرُ أَيْنَ قُمْنَا بِوَضْعِهَا."

"I think it's under my bed," said Jimmy. "I'll go check." With that, he ran inside the house, hoping to find the ball.

قَالَ جِيمِي : "أَعْتَقِدُ أَنَّهَا تَحْتَ سَرِيرِي، سَأَذْهَبُ لِأَتَأَكَّدَ مِنْ ذَلِكَ." ثُمَّ سَارَعَ نَحْوَ الْبَيْتِ آمِلًا أَنْ يَجِدَ الْكُرَةَ.

When he opened the door to their room he was very surprised. The floor was covered with puzzle pieces, building blocks, cars and other toys.

عِنْدَمَا فَتَحَ بَابَ غُرْفَته، تَفَاجَأَ كَثيرًا. كَانَتْ أَرْضِيَّةُ غُرْفتِه مُغَطَّاةً بِقِطع الْأُحْجِيَة و الْمُكَعَّبَاتِ الْخَشَبِيَّةِ، السَّيَّارَاتِ و الشَّاحِنَاتِ و أَلْعَابٌ أُخْرَى.

Eventually, he stumbled and lost his balance. He was trying to stay upright, but instead fell directly on his favorite train.

و فَجْأَةً ،تَعثَّر و فَقَدَ تَوازُنَهُ. حَاوَلَ أَنْ يَظِلَّ وَاقِفًا، و لَكِنَّهُ سَقَطَ عَلَى قِطَارِهِ الْمُفَضَّلِ.

"Ouch!" he screamed, watching the train's wheels flying in different direction. "Noooo, my train!" Jimmy burst into tears.

صَاحَ جِيمِي مُتَأَلِّمًا " آوتش!" و حِينَ رَأَى عَجَلَاتِ قِطَارِهِ تَتَطَايَرُ هُنَا و هُنَاكَ، قَالَ بَاكِيًا : " لَا ... قِطَارِي!"

"Are you alright, honey?" Dad appeared in the door. He couldn't fit inside the room due to all the mess.

دَخَلَ الْأَبُ قَائِلًا :" هَلْ أَنْتَ عَلَى مَا يُرَامُ يَا عَزِيزِي؟" و لَكِنَّهُ لَمْ يَسْتَطِعْ أَنْ يَدْخُلَ إِلَى الْغُرْفَةِ بِسَبَبِ الْفَوْضَى.

"I'm fine. But my train..." cried Jimmy, pointing to the train's broken wheels.

قَالَ جِيمِي بَاكِيًا و هُوَ يُشِيرُ إِلَى عَجَلَاتِ قِطَارِهِ الْمُحَطَّمَة :" أَنَا بِخَيْرٍ، و لكنْ قِطَارِي ..."

"I can't even see the train," said Dad. "And what exactly happened in this room?"

قَالَ الْأَبُ :" أَنَا لَا أَسْتَطِيعُ رُؤْيَةَ الْقِطَارِ أَصْلًا. مَاذَا حَصَلَ لِهَذِهِ الْغُرْفَةِ بِالضَّبْطِ؟"

"Jimmy, why's it taking you so long?" The other brothers' voices as they ran into the house.

قَالَ الْأَخَوَانِ الْأَكْبَرَانُ و هُمَا يَدْخُلَانِ الْبَيْتَ : "جِيمِي، لِماذَا تَأَخَّرْتَ ؟"

"My train broke!" Jimmy couldn't stop crying.

أَجَابَ جِيمِي و هُوَ لَمْ يَتَوَقَّفْ عَنِ الْبُكَاءِ بَعْدُ : " لَقَدْ تَكَسَّرَ قِطَارِي!"

"Don't cry, Jimmy," said the oldest brother. "We'll think of something. Dad?"

قَالَ الْأَخُ الأكبرُ: "لَا تَبْكِ يَا جِيمِي، سَنُفَكِّرُ فِي حَلٍّ مَا، مَا رَأْيُكَ يَا أَبِي؟"

"Maybe I could fix it," said Dad. "But you need to clean up in here. Bring me the train and the wheels after you find them". With that, Dad went out the room.

قَالَ الْأَبُ قَبْلَ أَنْ يُغَادِرَ الْغُرْفَةَ :" سَأَرَى إِنْ كُنْتُ قَادِرًا عَلَى إِصْلَاحِهِ. و لَكِنْ، عَلَيْكُمْ أَنْ تُرَتِّبُوا الْمَكَانَ، و بَعْدَ أَنْ تَجِدُوا الْقِطَارَ و الْعَجَلَاتِ، أَحْضِرُوهَا إِلَيَّ."

"We need to hurry, before Mom comes back," said the oldest brother.

قَالَ الْأَخُ الْأَكْبَرُ :" عَلَيْنَا أَنْ نُسْرِعَ قَبْلَ أَنْ تَأْتِيَ أُمِّي."

"Oh, cleaning up is boring," said Jimmy sighing and looking around the messy room.

فَقَالَ جِيمِي بِتَنَهُّدٍ و هُوَ يَجُوبُ بِنَظَرِه حَوْلَ الْغُرْفة الْفَوْضَوِيَّة :
" التّرْتِيبُ مُمِلٌّ . "

"Let's play a cleaning-up game then," exclaimed his oldest brother.

فَقَالَ الْأَخُ الْأَكْبَرُ مُتَعَجِّبًا :" فَلْنَلْعَبْ لُعْبَة التّنْظِيف إذَنْ."

Jimmy became excited. "The storm is coming soon!" he shouted. "We need to help all the toys get back to their houses."

تَحَمَّسَ جِيمِي فَصَاحَ :" سَتَأْتِي الْعَاصِفَةُ قَرِيبًا، عَلَيْنَا أَنْ نُسَاعِدَ
كُلَّ أَلْعَابِنَا و نُرْجِعَها إلَى دِيَارِهَا . "

"We're superheroes," yelled the middle brother. He picked up toys from the floor and put each one in its proper place.

صَاحَ الْأَخُ الْأَوْسَطُ : "نَحْنُ أَبْطَالٌ." ثُمَّ الْتَقَطَ أَلْعَابًا مِنَ الْأَرْضِ و وَضَعَ كُلَّ لُعْبَةٍ فِي مَكَانِهَا.

Playing and enjoying, the brothers organized and cleaned everything.

رَتَّبَ الْإِخْوَةُ الْمَكَانَ و هُمْ يَلْعَبُونَ و يَمْرَحُونَ.

"All wheels are here," exclaimed Jimmy, running to his father with the broken train in his hands.

" كُلُّ الْعَجَلَاتِ هُنَا،" هَتَفَ جِيمِي مُسْرِعًا نَحْوَ وَالِدِهِ و هُوَ يَحْمِلُ الْقِطَارَ الْمَكْسُورَ و عَجَلَاتِه بَيْنَ يَدَيْهِ.

"Here, I found the basketball!" screamed the middle brother with excitement.

صَاحَ الْأَخُ الْأَوْسَطُ مُتَحَمِّسًا :" انْظُرَا، لَقَدْ وَجَدْتُ كُرَةَ السَّلَّةِ!"

"Put it in its box and...we are finished," said the oldest brother happily.

قَالَ الْأَخُ الْأَكْبَرُ بِفَرَحٍ : "ضَعْهَا فِي الصُّنْدُوقِ، و بِذَلِكَ نَكُونُ قَدْ أَنْهَيْنَا مُهِمَّةَ التَّنْظِيفِ."

"It was really fun," said the middle brother, sitting down on his bed, "but it took us a whole hour."

قَالَ الْأَخُ الْأَوْسَطُ و هُوَ يَجْلِسُ عَلَى سَرِيرِهِ :" كَانَ ذَلِكَ مُمْتِعًا حَقًا، و لَكِنَّ التَّنْظِيفَ آسْتَغْرَقَ مِنَّا سَاعَةً كَامِلَةً."

"No!" yelled Jimmy as he entered the room.
"Don't sit there!"

صَاحَ جِيمِي و هُوَ يَدْخُلُ الْغُرْفَةَ :" لَا! لَا تَجْلِسْ هُنَاكَ!"

"What? Why?!" asked the middle brother,
jumping off the bed.

فَسَأَلَ الْأَخُ الْأَوْسَطُ قَافِزًا مِنْ عَلَى سَرِيرِه :" مَاذَا ؟ لِماذا ؟!"

"You just made your bed. If you sit on it now,
you'd have to make it again," explained Jimmy.

أَجَابَ جِيمِي مُفَسِّرًا :" لَقَدْ رَتَّبْتَ سَرِيرَكَ لِلتَّوِّ. اِذَا جَلَسْتَ عَلَيْهِ،
فَسَيَكُونُ عَلَيْكَ أَنْ تُرَتِّبَهُ مُجَدَّدًا."

"Maybe we could read a book now," suggested
the older brother, approaching the bookshelf.

اِقْتَرَحَ الْأَخُ الْأَكْبَرُ و هُوَ يَتَفَحَّصُ رَفَّ الْكُتُبِ :" مَا رَأْيُكُمَا أَنْ نَقْرَأَ كِتَابًا
الْآنَ؟"

"Don't touch those books," shouted Jimmy.
"I organized them all by color!"

فَصَاحَ جِيمِي :" لَا تَلْمَسْ تِلْكَ الْكُتُبَ، فَقَدْ رَتَّبْتُهَا كُلَّهَا حَسَبَ
الْأَلْوَانِ!"

"Sorry," said the oldest brother. "But what will we do? We can't play with anything."

قَالَ الْأَخُ الْأَكْبَرُ :" آسِف، ولكِنْ مَاذَا سنَفْعَلُ؟ أَلَنْ نَلْعَبَ شَيْئًا؟"

They thought for a while and then the oldest brother shouted: "I have an idea!"

فَكَّرَ الْإِخْوَةُ الثَّلَاثَةُ لِوَهْلَةٍ، ثُمَّ قَالَ الْأَخُ الْأَكْبَرُ :" عِنْدِي فِكْرَةٌ!"

"What if we clean up after each game?" he suggested. "Then it won't take so much time to put toys away."

"مَاذَا لَوْ رَتَّبْنَا الْمَكَانَ بَعْدَ كُلِّ لُعْبَةٍ نَلْعَبُهَا؟ إِذَا فَعَلْنَا ذَلِكَ، لَنْ يَسْتَغْرِقَ تَرْتِيبُ أَلْعَابِنَا وَقْتًا طَوِيلًا."

"Let's try," said Jimmy happily.

قَالَ جِيمِي فَرِحًا :" فِكْرَةٌ جَيِّدَةٌ، فَلْنُجَرِّبْهَا."

First, the oldest brother read a beautiful book to his younger brothers. When they finished reading, he put it back on the shelf.

أَوَّلًا ، قَرَأَ الْأَخُ الْأَكْبَرُ لِأَخَوَيْهِ كِتَابًا جَمِيلًا، و بَعْدَ أَنْ أَنْهَى ثَلَاثَتُهُمُ الْقِرَاءَةَ، أَعَادَ الْكِتَابَ إِلَى مَكَانِهِ.

Next, they built a large tower out of their colorful blocks. When they were done, they put the blocks back into the box — and the room stayed clean!

وَ بَعْدَ ذَلِكَ، بَنَوْا حِصْنًا كَبِيرًا بِمُكَعَّبَاتِهِمْ الْمُلَوَّنَة الْخَشَبِيَّة، وَ حِينَ انْتَهَوْا مِنْها، أَعَادُوَاهَا إِلَى صُنْدُوقِهَا، وَ بَقِيَتِ الْغُرْفَةُ نَظِيفَةً!

At that moment, Mom and Dad knocked on the door.

فِي تِلْكَ اللَّحْظَةِ، طَرَقَ الْأَبُ وَ الْأُمُّ الْبَابَ.

"I missed you so much," said Mom, "but I see you managed to keep your room clean. I'm so proud of you."

قَالَتِ الْأُمُّ :" لَقَدِ اشْتَقْتُ إِلَيْكُمْ كَثِيرًا. لَاحَظْتُ أَنَّكُمْ تَمَكَّنْتُم مِن الْحِفَاظِ عَلَى غُرْفَتِكُمْ جَمِيلَةً وَ مُرَتَّبَةً، أَنَا فَخُورَةٌ جِدًّا بِكُمْ."

"And here's your train, Jimmy," said Dad, handing him the toy. The wheels were fixed and Jimmy smiled widely.

قَالَ الْأَبُ وَ هُوَ يُعْطِي الْقِطَارَ لِجِيمِي :" هَاهُوَ ذَا قِطَارُكَ يَا جِيمِي." لَقَدْ تَمَكَّنَ الْأَبُ مِنْ إِصْلَاحِ الْعَجَلَاتِ، فَارْتَسَمَتْ عَلَى وَجْهِ جِيمِي ابْتِسَامَةٌ وَاسِعَةٌ.

"Who wants to try cookies that Granny made for you?" asked Mom.

سَأَلَتِ الْأُمُّ الْجَمِيعَ :" مَنْ يَرْغَبُ فِي تَذَوُّقِ الْكَعْكِ الَّذِي حَضَّرَتْهُ جَدَّتَكُمْ لَكُمْ ؟"

"Me!" shouted the bunny brothers and their Dad.

صَاحَ الْأَبُ و الْأَطْفَالُ :" أَنَا!"

"But we'll eat them in the kitchen, not in this clean room," said Jimmy very seriously. "Right, Mom?"

قَالَ جِيمِي بِجِدِّيَّةٍ :" و لَكِنَّا سَنَتَنَاوَلُهَا فِي الْمَطْبَخِ و لَيْسَ فِي هَذِهِ الْغُرْفَةِ النَّظِيفَةِ، أَلَيْسَ كَذَلِكَ يَا أُمِّي؟"

The whole family started laughing loudly and went to the kitchen to eat cookies.

ضَحِكَ الْجَمِيعُ عَالِيًا، ثُمَّ ذَهَبُوا إِلَى الْمَطْبَخِ لِتَنَاوُلِ الْكَعْكِ.

Since that day, the brothers loved to keep their room clean and organized. They played with all their toys but when they finished, they put everything back in its place.

و مُنْذَ ذَلِكَ الْيَوْمِ ، حَرِصَ الْأَطْفَالُ عَلَى الْمُحَافَظَةِ عَلَى نَظَافَةِ غُرْفَتِهِمْ، و أَصْبَحُوا يُعِيدُونَ كُلَّ قِطَعِ الْأَلْعَابِ إِلَى مَكَانِهَا كُلَّمَا آنْتَهُوا مِنَ اللَّعِبِ.

It never took them long to clean up their room again.

وَ لَمْ يَسْتَغْرِقْ تَرْتِيبُ غُرْفَتِهِمْ وَقْتًا طَوِيلًا مِنْ بَعْدِ ذَلِكَ أَبَدًا.

CPSIA information can be obtained
at www.ICGtesting.com
Printed in the USA
LVHW07*1708060918
589366LV00029B/547/P